D1626665

All About Plants

All About
Stems

Claire Throp

Raintree is an imprint of Capstone Global Library Limited,
a company incorporated in England and Wales having
its registered office at 7 Pilgrim Street, London, EC4V 6LB –
Registered company number: 6695582

www.raintreepublishers.co.uk
myorders@raintreepublishers.co.uk

Text © Capstone Global Library Limited 2015
First published in hardback in 2014
The moral rights of the proprietor have been asserted.

Edited by Claire Throp and Brynn Baker
Designed by Peggie Carley
Picture research by Ruth Blair
Production by Victoria Fitzgerald
Originated by Capstone Global Library Ltd
Printed and bound in China by RR Donnelley Asia

ISBN 978 1 406 28441 6
18 17 16 15 14
10 9 8 7 6 5 4 3 2 1

British Library Cataloguing in Publication Data
A full catalogue record for this book is available from the
British Library.

Acknowledgements
We would like to thank the following for permission to
reproduce photographs: Dreamstime: Erikamariag2,
7; Getty Images: WIN-Initiative, 21; iStockphoto: Kurt
Drubbel, 11; Shutterstock: Arevik, 14, Filipe B. Varela,
5, gemphoto, 17, gillmar, 8, Igor Borodin, 18, Jane
McLoughlin, 19, Krzysztof Wiktor, 20, Maria Skaldina, 6,
23 (top), Max Topchii, cover, Mikhail Dudarev, 4, mythja,
16, 23 (bottom), Rafal Olechowski, 9, Scott Sanders,
back cover, 15, 23 (middle), Serg64, 13, smuay, 10, Steve
Slocomb, 12, StudioNewmarket, 22.

We would like to thank Michael Bright for his invaluable
help in the preparation of this book.

Every effort has been made to contact copyright
holders of material reproduced in this book. Any
omissions will be rectified in subsequent printings if
notice is given to the publisher.

Contents

What are plants?

Plants are living things.

flower

stem

leaf

root

seed

Plants have
many parts.

What do plants need to grow?

Plants need sunlight and **air** to grow.

Plants need water to grow.

What are stems?

stem

seed

Stems grow from the seeds
of plants.

Most stems grow above the ground.
Stems help to hold up a plant.

Stems move water and food
around a plant.

Flowers and leaves grow
from stems.

Types of stems

Some plants have thick stems.

Some plants have thin stems.

Some plants have flat stems.

Some plants have **thorny** stems.

Some plants have **woody** stems.
A tree trunk is a stem.

Some plants have smooth stems.

stem

Some stems grow along the ground.
Strawberry stems grow like this.

stem

Many stems grow straight up.
Rhubarb stems grow like this.

Stems as food

Some animals like to eat stems.

Some people like to eat stems too.
Asparagus is a stem.

Plants need stems

Stems hold up plants.

Stems move food around plants.

Picture glossary

 air oxygen people, plants, and animals breathe to live

 thorny many sharp, prickly points on a plant

 woody made of wood

Index

Notes for parents and teachers

Before reading

Ask children if they know what stems are for. Explain that plant stems can look very different from one another. For example, strawberry runners and tree trunks are very different.

After reading

- Ask children to say what grows from a stem.
- See if children can remember what three things plants need most to survive. (pages 6 and 7)
- Demonstrate how water moves through stems. Use a white carnation with a freshly cut stem. Put the flower in a vase with water and food colouring. Ask children to predict what will happen. The coloured water will be absorbed by the stem and travel up to the petals. The flower will change colour.